CRAYOLA
OUTSIDE
CRAFTS

Rebecca Felix

LERNER PUBLICATIONS ◆ MINNEAPOLIS

The photographs in this book were created by Mighty Media, Inc.

Official Licensed Product
Lerner Publications Company
A division of Lerner Publishing Group, Inc.
241 First Avenue North
Minneapolis, MN 55401 USA

For reading levels and more information, look up this title at www.lernerbooks.com.

Main body text set in Mikado a 14/19.
Typeface provided by HVD Fonts.

Library of Congress Cataloging-in-Publication Data

Names: Felix, Rebecca, 1984- author. | Crayola (Firm)
Title: Crayola outside crafts / by Rebecca Felix.
Description: Minneapolis : Lerner Publications, 2019. | Series: Colorful
    Crayola crafts | Includes bibliographical references and index. | Audience:
    Ages 6–10. | Audience: K to Grade 3.
Identifiers: LCCN 2018014661 (print) | LCCN 2018028141 (ebook) |
    ISBN 9781541512498 (eb pdf) | ISBN 9781541510975 (lb : alk. paper) |
    ISBN 9781541545977 (pb : alk. paper)
Subjects: LCSH: Handicraft for children—Juvenile literature. | Nature
    observation—Juvenile literature.
Classification: LCC TT160 (ebook) | LCC TT160 .F4574 2019 (print) |
    DDC 745.5083—dc23

LC record available at https://lccn.loc.gov/2018014661

Manufactured in the United States of America
1-43981-33995-9/26/2018

Contents

Scan QR codes throughout for step-by-step photos of each craft.

GET CREATIVE OUTSIDE!

Are you a maker? You can be! Follow the steps to make amazing outdoor crafts.

Let the photos and colorful materials inspire you. Get ready to create outdoors!

Crafting Safety

▶ **Plan ahead** before creating outside! Look at the weather forecast. Then dress appropriately. This may mean wearing boots, comfortable shoes, a jacket, and more.

▶ **Bring and use safety items** as needed when crafting outdoors. This can include sunscreen, bug spray, and drinking water.

▶ **Ask an adult** for permission before using sharp tools, bringing craft supplies outdoors, and using materials you've found outside.

▶ **Use plastic containers** instead of glass. Glass can break if it is dropped on a paved driveway, sidewalk, or rocky surface.

Outside Tips

▶ Keep workspaces and crafts clean.

　　■ Cover outdoor workspaces with a tarp or old towel or sheet.

▶ Think about the weather when preparing supplies.

　　■ Is it hot and sunny? Keep any electronic craft tools in the shade to keep them from overheating.

　　■ Is it windy? Keep lightweight materials such as feathers in a closed container to keep them from blowing away.

▶ Respect nature!

　　■ Leave no trace of your crafting behind outside. Pick up all materials and supplies. Clean any spilled paint or glue as best you can.

TINTED TREE

Create a colorful autumn tree that will last all year!

Materials
- leaves
- crayons
- paper
- scissors
- large piece of paper
- glue

1. Gather leaves outdoors.

2. Peel the paper labels off the crayons.

3. Place a leaf under a piece of paper. Hold the leaf in place, and rub the length of a crayon over it across the paper. You'll see the leaf's outline and features appear!

4. Make many leaf rubbings. Cut them out.

3.

4.

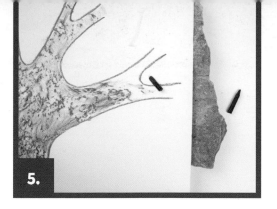

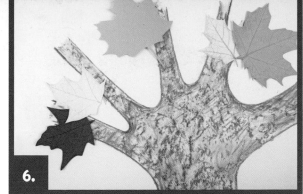

5. Draw a tree trunk and branches on a large sheet of paper. Create a real-looking trunk by making a bark rubbing! Hold the page against a tree trunk or stone, and rub inside the trunk and branch lines with crayon.

6. Glue the leaves to the tree branches. Glue some leaves in the center of the page or at the base of the trunk. These are fallen leaves!

Scan code to see more photos!

EARTH PATTERNS PAINTING

Make a painting featuring a natural pattern!

Materials

- notebook and colored pencils or digital camera or smartphone
- card stock
- paint
- paintbrushes
- scissors
- cardboard
- dark marker (optional)
- glue

1. Explore your neighborhood to search for patterns in nature! This could be the pattern on a butterfly wing, a flower petal, or a bird's feathers. Patterns are also found in spiderwebs, leaves, honeycombs, and much more!

2. If you are using a notebook, draw any patterns you find using colored pencils. If you are using a digital camera or smartphone, take photos of patterns you see.

3. Review the patterns from step 2. Choose one pattern and re-create it on the card stock using paint. Let the paint dry.

4. Cut a piece of cardboard a bit larger than the card stock. Paint one side a bright color. Let the paint dry.

5. If your painted pattern is blurring together, use a dark marker to outline the pattern.

6. Use a clean paintbrush to brush glue on the back of the card stock. Glue it in the center of the cardboard. Trim the cardboard into a frame. Then hang your painting in your home to enjoy nature's patterns indoors!

Tip:
Some patterns are made up of shapes. But colors can also make a pattern! Look for stripes or other colors that repeat in an order.

NATURE MASK

Gather materials from nature and make a mask!

Materials

- lightweight natural objects, such as leaves, acorns, shells, grasses, feathers, seeds, or flower petals
- scissors
- empty cereal box
- pencil
- paint
- paintbrush
- tape
- glue
- crayons
- duct tape
- large stick or craft stick

2.

1. Gather lightweight, natural objects from outdoors. This could be leaves, acorns, or grasses. Feathers, seeds, and flower petals also work well.

2. Cut along one long edge of the cereal box to create a flat sheet of cardboard. Draw and cut out a mask shape on the cardboard. Cut out a horizontal rectangle on each side of the mask as eyeholes.

3. Paint the mask, and let it dry.

4. Tape and glue the natural objects you gathered to the mask. Let the glue dry.

5. Draw shapes or designs on the mask using crayons.

6. Use duct tape to attach the large stick to the back of the mask as a handle. Use the handle to hold the mask in front of your face!

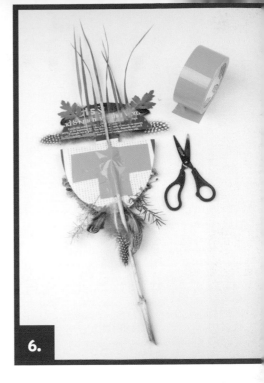

6.

NEIGHBORHOOD MOSAIC

Mosaics are artworks made from small, colorful shapes formed into designs or patterns. Make a mosaic that represents shapes in your neighborhood!

Materials

- notebook and pencil or digital camera or smartphone
- thin cardboard
- scissors
- construction paper
- paint
- paintbrushes
- thick sheet of cardboard
- glue stick

1. Explore your neighborhood! Bring a notebook and pencil or digital camera or smartphone. Look for geometric shapes on buildings, sidewalks, roads, and signs. These might be square windows or rectangular bricks. You may see a hexagonal sign. Sketch or take photos of the shapes you see.

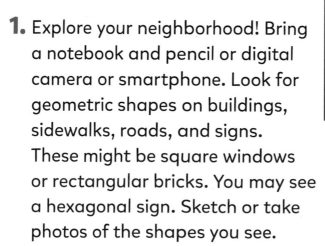

2. Redraw the shapes you saw on thin cardboard. Cut out the shapes.

3. Trace the cutouts on colorful construction paper. Cut out the shapes.

4. Paint one side of the thick cardboard. Let the paint dry.

5. Glue the paper cutouts to the cardboard. Arrange them close together, but not touching. Hang your neighborhood mosaic indoors!

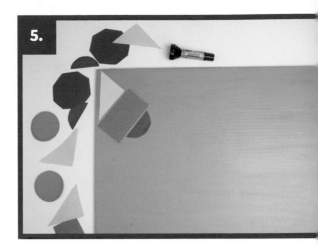

CREATURE CREATION

Make animals designed to survive outdoors where you live!

Materials

- notebook
- pencil
- large sheet of paper
- paint
- paintbrushes
- construction paper
- markers
- scissors
- tape
- glue

1. Go outside and study the environment. Take notes on what you see and feel. Think about these questions:

- Is there water nearby?

- Is there snow?

- Do you see tall grass, trees, or mountains?

- Do you see any animals?

2. On a large sheet of paper, paint the environment you studied.

3. Use your notes to brainstorm the features animals should have to survive in the environment. This might be thick fur to stay warm or hooves to climb mountains.

4. On construction paper, draw and color different body parts for each feature from step 3. These will be put together to form new made-up animals. Depending on the features you wrote down, you may end up with more than one set of feet, ears, or other body parts. That is okay! But make sure you have at least one body and one head for each animal.

5. Cut out all body parts from step 4. Then tape and glue the pieces together to create unique animals! Add details with markers.

6. Glue the animals to the habitat. Cut a frame from construction paper, and tape it to the back of the painting. Then hang your creature creation on the wall!

CONSTELLATION ART

Study the stars. Then re-create them in a glittery work of art!

Materials
- notepad
- pencil
- flashlight or lantern
- black construction paper
- glitter glue
- paintbrush
- chalk
- poster board
- scissors
- glue

1. With an adult's permission, go outdoors at night to view the stars. Bring a notepad, a pencil, and a lantern or flashlight. Then study the stars! Look for constellations, and draw them on the paper.

2. Back inside, squirt dark-colored glitter glue on the black construction paper. Use a paintbrush to spread the glitter glue across the page. Let the glue dry.

2.

3. Use bright-colored glitter glue to re-create the constellations on the black paper.

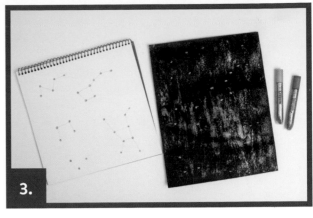

4. Use chalk to connect the stars in each constellation to set them apart.

5. Cut out a piece of poster board as a frame. Glue the constellation art to the frame. Then hang your creation indoors to see the stars any time of the day!

Tip:
Add a glow-in-the-dark moon or stars to bring some light to your painting.

BUG JARS

Build jar habitats to keep clay insects indoors!

Materials

- insects (optional)
- pencil
- notebook
- a variety of natural objects, such as twigs, leaves, grass, moss, and stones
- small bowl
- water
- air-dry clay
- toothpicks
- paint
- paintbrushes
- scissors
- glue
- clear, plastic jars with lids

1. Hunt for insects outdoors! Don't catch them. Just study and describe the insects in a notebook. If you don't see any insects, it's okay! Move on to step 2.

2. Gather twigs, leaves, grass, moss, stones, and other natural objects.

2.

3. Fill a small bowl with water. Then create the insects you saw using clay and toothpicks. If you didn't see any insects, research them online or in a book. Use the water to keep the clay wet while working. Let the clay dry overnight.

4.

4. Paint the insects, and let the paint dry.

5. Arrange the items from step 2 inside the jars. If the twigs are long, cut off their ends until they can fit inside the jar.

6. Glue each insect to a twig. Let the glue dry, and place the twigs inside the jars. Then put your bug jars on display!

WILD WEATHER MOBILES

Make outdoor decorations to reflect the local weather!

Materials
- pencil
- construction paper
- scissors
- packaging tape
- hole punch
- fishing line or string
- markers
- small, lightweight natural objects such as leaves, pinecones, or flowers

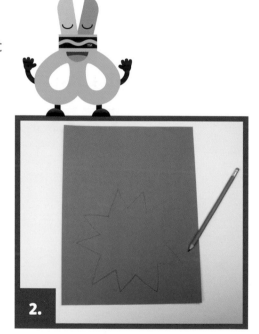

2.

1. Think about the weather where you live. Is it often rainy, sunny, or snowy? Does the weather change with the seasons?

2. Choose a type of weather. Then draw either a cloud or sunburst on construction paper.

3.

3. Cut out the shape from step 2. If you made a sunburst, cut out two circles and glue them to either side of the sun shape.

4. Cover both sides of it in strips of tape. This makes the shape waterproof! Trim off any extra tape.

5. Punch three holes near the bottom edge of the shape. Punch one hole in the top of the shape.

4.

Wild Weather Mobiles
continued next page

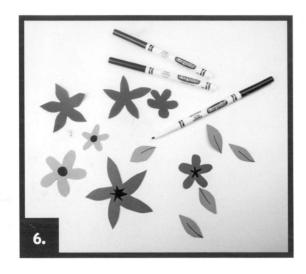

6.

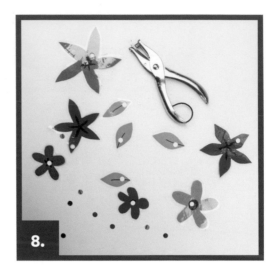

8.

6. Draw and cut out raindrops, snowflakes, leaves, or flowers from construction paper. Decorate them with markers.

7. Repeat step 4 to waterproof the small shapes.

8. Punch a hole in each shape from step 6.

9. Cut four lengths of fishing line or string about 2 feet (0.6 meters) long. Tie one to the top hole in the sun or cloud to make a loop for hanging. Tie one end of each of the other strings to the bottom holes.

10. Tie the shapes from step 6 to the strings. Tie a flower, branch, or other natural object to the end of each string.

11. Hang your mobile outside! Change out the natural elements whenever you like or as the season changes.

10.

TREE OF LIFE

Create a small tree full of colorful animals and plants!

Materials

- pencil
- notebook
- Model Magic
- scissors
- construction paper
- stapler
- branch with several smaller branches
- glue
- small flowerpot
- sand or gravel
- rocks
- floral wire

1. Research what animals live in trees. Write down a list. Include animals that perch in trees or climb them for food.

2. Make the animals from step 1 using Model Magic! Let the animals dry overnight.

3. Cut leaves from construction paper. Gather the leaves in small bunches, and staple them together.

4. Gather a large branch from outdoors. Make sure it has several smaller branches. Strip the branch of its leaves. Trim the branches if they are long.

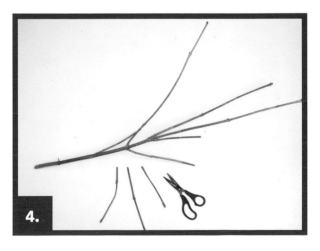

Tree of Life
continued next page

5. Glue the leaf bunches to the ends of the branches. Let the glue dry.

6. Fill the flowerpot with sand or gravel. Push the branch into the sand or gravel so it stands upright like a tree. Add rocks to the pot to help hold the branch in place.

5.

6.

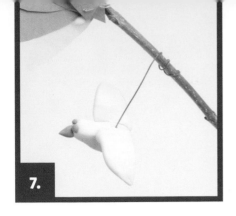

7.

9.

7. Cut a piece of floral wire. Stick it into a flying animal. Twist the other end of the wire around a branch.

8. Repeat step 7 for all flying animals.

9. Glue some animals to the branches or vase. Then display your tree indoors. Change out or make more animals whenever you like or as the seasons change!

Get Creative!

Look at materials, steps, and craft photos. Are you missing some materials to re-create a craft? Would you have done the craft differently? Try it out!

Find new ways to make each project your own. Try using real flowers and leaves instead of paper, or swap out markers for glitter glue. Make many nature masks and put on a play, or create a cactus instead of a tree and fill it with clay desert critters! With art supplies and some imagination, the possibilities are endless.

Glossary

appropriately: suitable for the situation you are in

constellation: a group of stars that forms a shape or figure and usually has a name

designed: drawn or planned

features: parts or details that stand out

geometric: of or having to do with geometry, which is the branch of mathematics that deals with points, lines, angles, shapes, and solids

habitat: the place where an animal or a plant is usually found

hexagonal: having a shape of a hexagon, or with six straight sides

honeycombs: wax structures made by bees to store honey and pollen and to raise young bees. A honeycomb is made up of many rows of hexagonal shapes.

mobiles: artistic structures that are moved easily or that have parts easily moved

mosaic: a pattern or picture made up of small, colored pieces

research: to collect information about a subject

To Learn More

Books

Felix, Rebecca. *Duct Tape Survival Gear*. Minneapolis: Lerner Publications, 2017.
Learn how to turn duct tape into all sorts of working items. Make a simple water glass, cast, net, and even a full-sized hammock!

Heinecke, Liz Lee. *Outdoor Science Lab for Kids: 52 Family-Friendly Experiments for the Yard, Garden, Playground, and Park*. Beverly, MA: Quarry Books, 2016.
Find projects that relate to all types of science topics and can be completed at home, in a backyard, or even on the playground. Then get ready to experiment, craft, and create!

Thompson, Veronica. *Earth-Friendly Earth Day Crafts*. Minneapolis: Lerner Publications, 2019.
Celebrate the great outdoors with these fun and easy Earth Day crafts.

Websites

Rockin' Rocks Sculpture
http://www.crayola.com/crafts/rockin-rock-sculpture-craft/
Paint gathered stones with bright designs. Then stack them into small sculptures!

17 Nature-Inspired Crafts for Kids
https://www.parents.com/fun/arts-crafts/kid/nature-inspired-crafts-ideas-for-kids/
Visit this website to find photos and step-by-step directions for creating all kinds of crafts using natural items gathered outdoors!

Index